Poptropica®

The Ultimate Guide

Elizabeth Corfe

Contents

Welcome to Poptropica®!

Who wants to trek through the African desert to find missing jewels? Who wants to gather clues to solve puzzles and mysteries?

Poptropica
EXPLORE · COLLECT · COMPETE
NEW PLAYER
RETURNING PLAYER
VIDEOS
CREATORS' BLOG!
MEMBERSHIP & CREDITS
MEMBERSHIP TOUR
MERCHANDISE
NEW ISLAND NOTICE

Welcome to Poptropica – a **virtual world** where you can meet friends, crack mysteries and test your skills against other **Poptropicans**.

Poptropica
UH, SO WHAT DO WE DO NEXT?
SO WHAT'S THE HOLD UP?
WHAT'S INSIDE THE TOMB?
Save and Quit

Are You Ready?

Have your wits about you – Poptropica is full of surprises. With more than ten islands to discover in the virtual world of Poptropica, there's a challenge on every corner.

Poptropica
BOBO'S
CLOWN STORE
OPEN

Along the way, you will make new friends and join in head-to-head battles in games like "Hoops" and "Paint War". If you're clever you can even solve the islands' **missions** and win cool medallions!

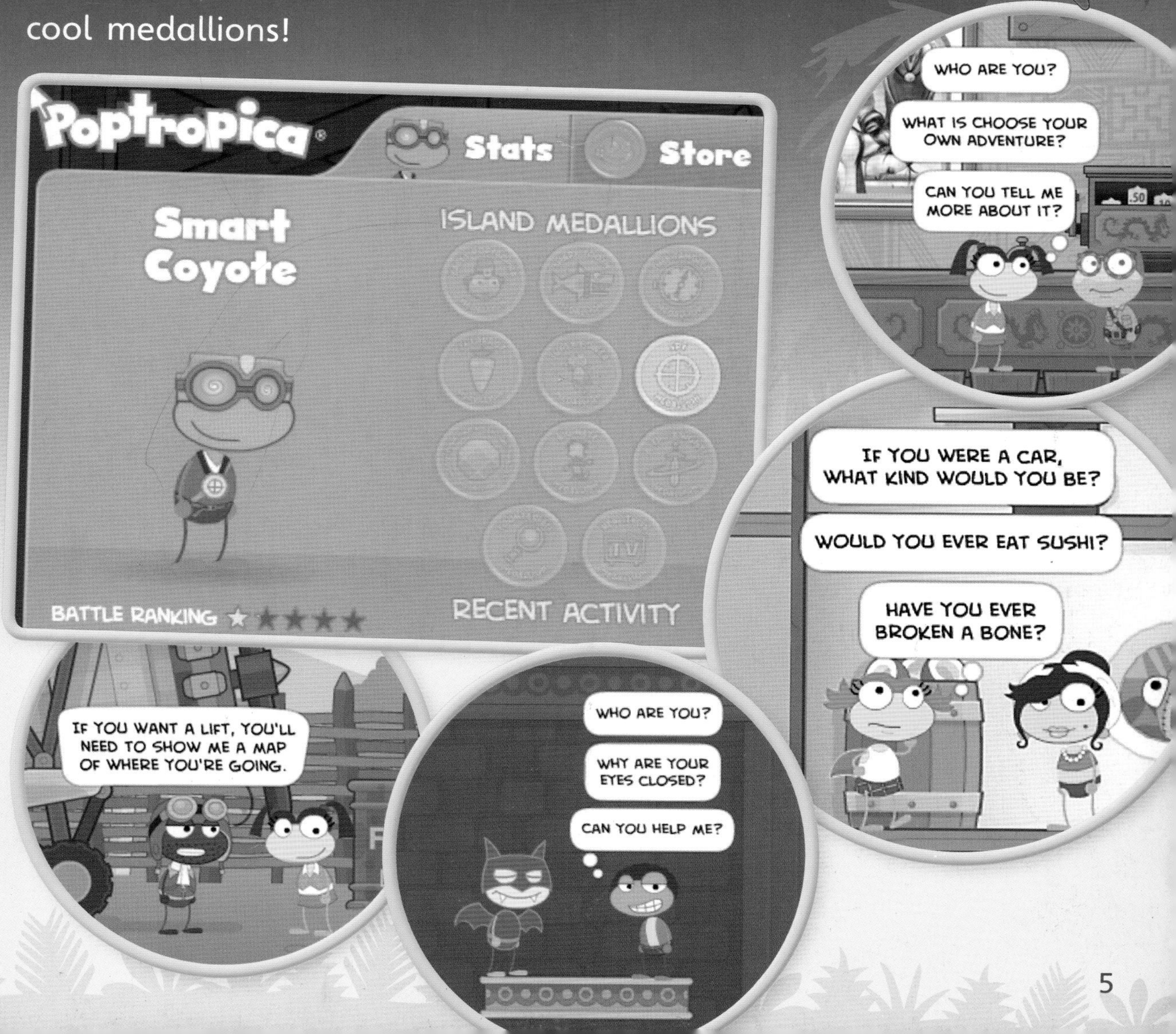

Poptropica
Stats
Store
Smart Coyote
ISLAND MEDALLIONS
BATTLE RANKING
RECENT ACTIVITY
WHO ARE YOU?
WHAT IS CHOOSE YOUR OWN ADVENTURE?
CAN YOU TELL ME MORE ABOUT IT?
IF YOU WERE A CAR, WHAT KIND WOULD YOU BE?
WOULD YOU EVER EAT SUSHI?
HAVE YOU EVER BROKEN A BONE?
IF YOU WANT A LIFT, YOU'LL NEED TO SHOW ME A MAP OF WHERE YOU'RE GOING.
WHO ARE YOU?
WHY ARE YOUR EYES CLOSED?
CAN YOU HELP ME?

Your Guide

Whether you are new to Poptropica, or a big fan already, this book is your guide to everything Poptropica.

This book will:

- ✔ Make you a Poptropica expert.
- ✔ Give you inside information on the islands.
- ✔ Give you secret tips to make your Poptropican even better!

This book won't:

- ✘ Do your maths homework.
- ✘ Turn your brother into an orang-utan.

Did you know?

Everyone in Poptropica travels by **blimp**.

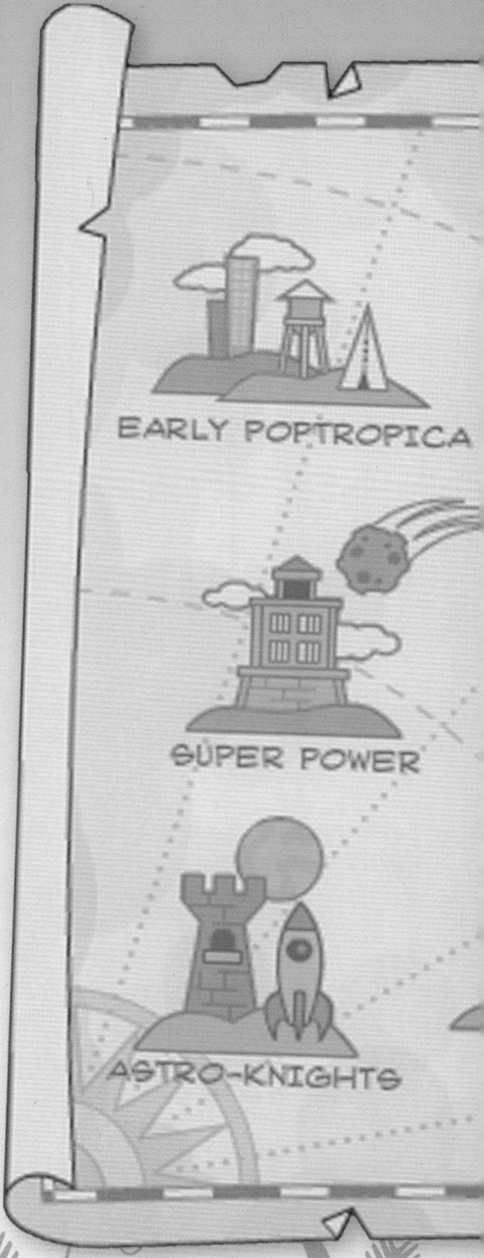
EARLY POPTROPICA
SUPER POWER
ASTRO-KNIGHTS

Poptropica
Select an island
HARK TOOTH
TIME TANGLED
24 CARROT
SPY
BIG NATE
CHOOSE YOUR OWN ADVENTURE
NABOOTI
TERFEIT
REALITY TV
MYTHOLOGY

Screen Play

There's no limit to what you can do in virtual worlds. Want to climb Mount Everest? No problem. Fancy exploring the pyramids in Egypt? Easy.

A virtual world is a place you can go to on the internet to chat, explore and play games against other users. It's like a world inside the world of computers.

Poptropica
EXPLORE · COLLECT · COMPETE
NEW PLAYER
RETURNING PLAYER

Amazing Avatars

First things first. Before you set off on your Poptropica adventures, you need an **avatar** (say *av-uh-tah*) – an **online** you.

In Poptropica, you're given your avatar, or Poptropican, when you first log in. You could be anything from Eagle Girl to Giant Brain to Fierce Dragon!

Yellow Socks

Young Sky

Poptropic
WELCOME TO POPTROPICA!
Happy Mosquito
CHANGE ALL
SKIN COLOR
HAIR
HAIR COLOR
EYES
MOUTH
SHIRT
PANTS
VIDEOS
CREATORS' BLOG!
MEMBERSHIP & CREDITS
MEMBERSHIP TOUR
MERCHANDISE

Happy Runner
Slippery Runner
Gentle Shell
Noisy Leaf
Crazy Grape
Greedy Whale
Jumpy Pear
Bony Shark

Now, choose your look – maybe red wavy hair with a big wide smile.

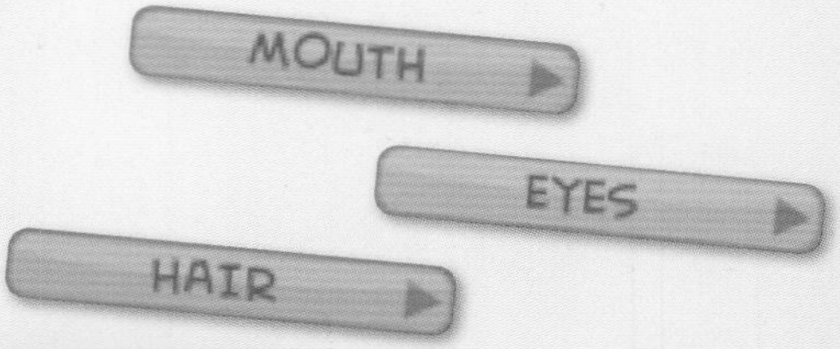
MOUTH
EYES
HAIR

Green Spinner
Green Spinner
Green Spinner
Green Spinner

Next, choose your clothes and you're ready to go! You can change what you look like whenever you want.

SPOTTED CHEETAH
SPOTTED CHEETAH
SPOTTED CHEETAH
SPOTTED CHEETAH
SPOTTED CHEETAH

Down to Business

Virtual worlds aren't just about fun. Businesses use virtual worlds to hold meetings and sell their goods.

Some schools are virtual! Children who can't get to an actual school go to school online.

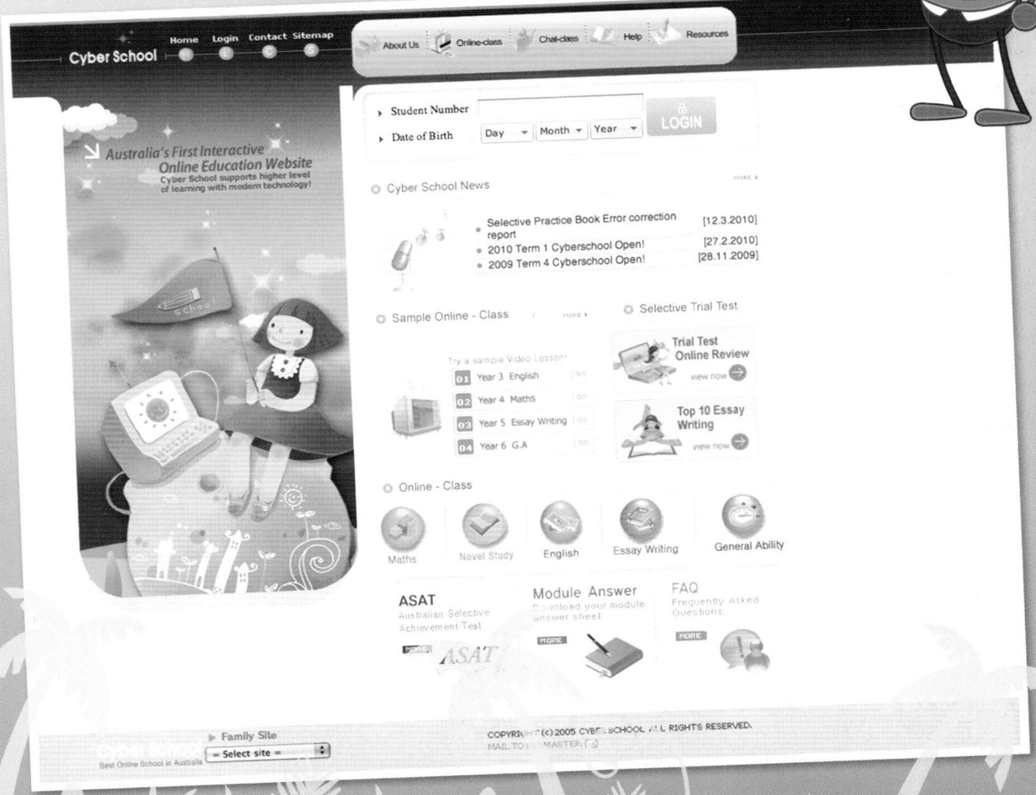
Cyber School
Home
Login
Contact
Sitemap
About Us
Online-class
Chat-class
Help
Resources
Student Number
Date of Birth
Day
Month
Year
LOGIN
Australia's First Interactive Online Education Website
Cyber School supports higher level of learning with modern technology!
Cyber School News
Selective Practice Book Error correction report [12.3.2010]
2010 Term 1 Cyberschool Open! [27.2.2010]
2009 Term 4 Cyberschool Open! [28.11.2009]
Sample Online - Class
Try a sample Video Lesson!
01 Year 3 English
02 Year 4 Maths
03 Year 5 Essay Writing
04 Year 6 G.A
Selective Trial Test
Trial Test Online Review
view now
Top 10 Essay Writing
view now
Online - Class
Maths
Novel Study
English
Essay Writing
General Ability
ASAT
Australian Selective Achievement Test
MORE
ASAT
Module Answer
answer sheet
MORE
FAQ
Frequently Asked Questions
MORE
Family Site
= Select site =
Best Online School in Australia

Don't Forget!

Virtual worlds are excellent places to explore and have fun. Some virtual worlds, like Poptropica, are more child-friendly than others.

Play it safe. Always follow these guidelines when you log on to a virtual world.

Do!

- Check with an adult before you play – are they okay with you entering that site?

Don't!

- Share **personal information** online! This includes stuff like your real name, your phone number, your school and address.

Do!

- Tell an adult if someone is asking personal questions, being rude or making you feel uncomfortable.

Explore Poptropica®

Shark Tooth Island

Something fishy is going on at Shark Tooth Island – a fierce shark called Booga is making trouble. To save the island and **defeat** the giant shark, you'll need to find the **concoction** hidden in the ruins. Can you do it?

SHARK
MUSEUM
THAT BEASTLY SHARK SURE HAS MADE A MESS OF THINGS OVER ON BOOGA BAY!
Poptropica

JOURNAL

Astro-Knights

Disaster has struck! Poptropicans want you to rescue their king and queen from outer space. You'll need to make your own spaceship and explore weird planets. Are you up for the challenge?

Poptropica

Time Tangled Island

The future is all messed up and needs your help. Go back in time and set things straight. You'll have to gather clues and speak with well-known people from the past to fix things. Good luck!

LAB
1776 AD

I'M BENJAMIN FRANKLIN. I WONDER WHAT'S TAKING JEFFERSON SO LONG IN THERE!
I'M THOMAS EDISON. I'M AN INVENTOR.

Spy Island

Poptropicans are losing their hair, three important spies are missing and a shady organisation called B.A.D is up to no good. Will you save the day?

B.A.D
BISTRO
OPEN LATE!
B.A.D
B.A.D

Extra Stuff

Give your Poptropican a pumpkin head, a jester's hat or a cowgirl outfit. Poptropica **credits** get you new **accessories** and special powers like shrinking and freezing time.

Poptropica Store

In Poptropica, you can buy credits or earn them as you complete the islands.

Poptropica
Stats
Store
Stuff
CLOSE
MEMBERSHIP:
BUY
CREDITS: 25
BUY MORE
GOLD CARDS
Followers
Time Freeze
Balloons
Torch
CREATE
PUT ON
INFLATE
TORCH
COSTUMES
NEWEST | MOST POPULAR | CREATORS' PICKS | VIEW ALL | LIST VIEW

Fact Monsters

Learn cool facts from the Fact Monsters. They give you extra information about the people you meet and the places you go.

Fact Monster

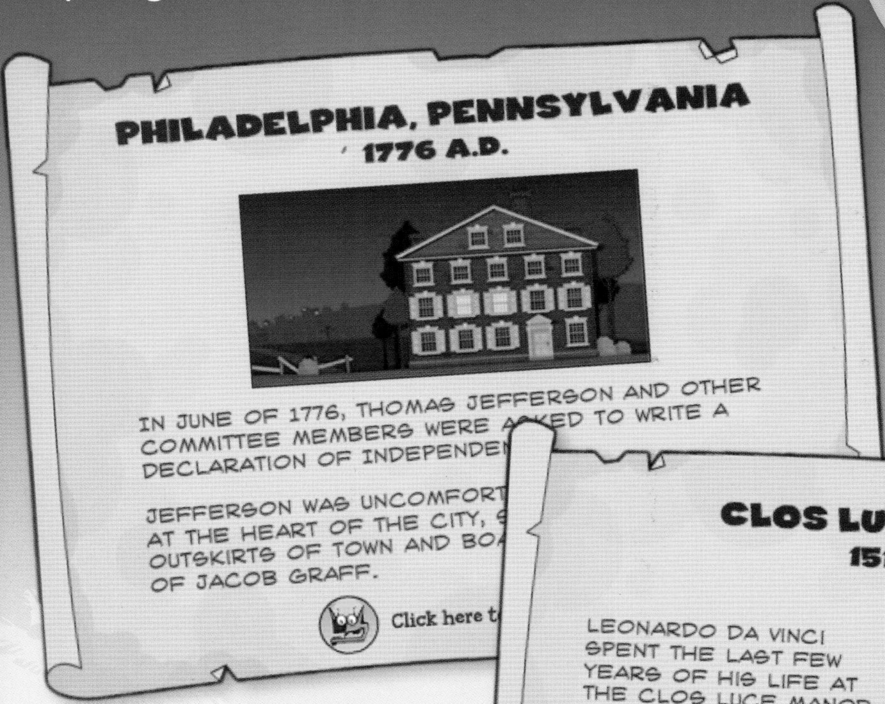
PHILADELPHIA, PENNSYLVANIA
1776 A.D.
IN JUNE OF 1776, THOMAS JEFFERSON AND OTHER
COMMITTEE MEMBERS WERE
DECLARATION OF INDEPENDE
JEFFERSON WAS UNCOMFORT
AT THE HEART OF THE CITY,
OUTSKIRTS OF TOWN AND BO
OF JACOB GRAFF.
Click here t

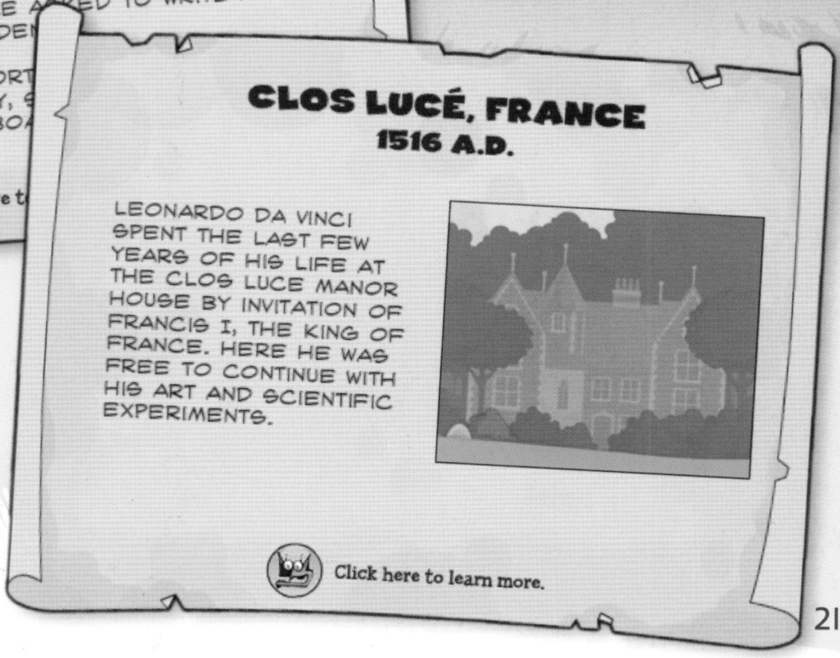
CLOS LUCÉ, FRANCE
1516 A.D.
LEONARDO DA VINCI SPENT THE LAST FEW YEARS OF HIS LIFE AT THE CLOS LUCE MANOR HOUSE BY INVITATION OF FRANCIS I, THE KING OF FRANCE. HERE HE WAS FREE TO CONTINUE WITH HIS ART AND SCIENTIFIC EXPERIMENTS.
Click here to learn more.

The Inside Scoop

Meet one of the makers of Poptropica, Director D from Spy Island.

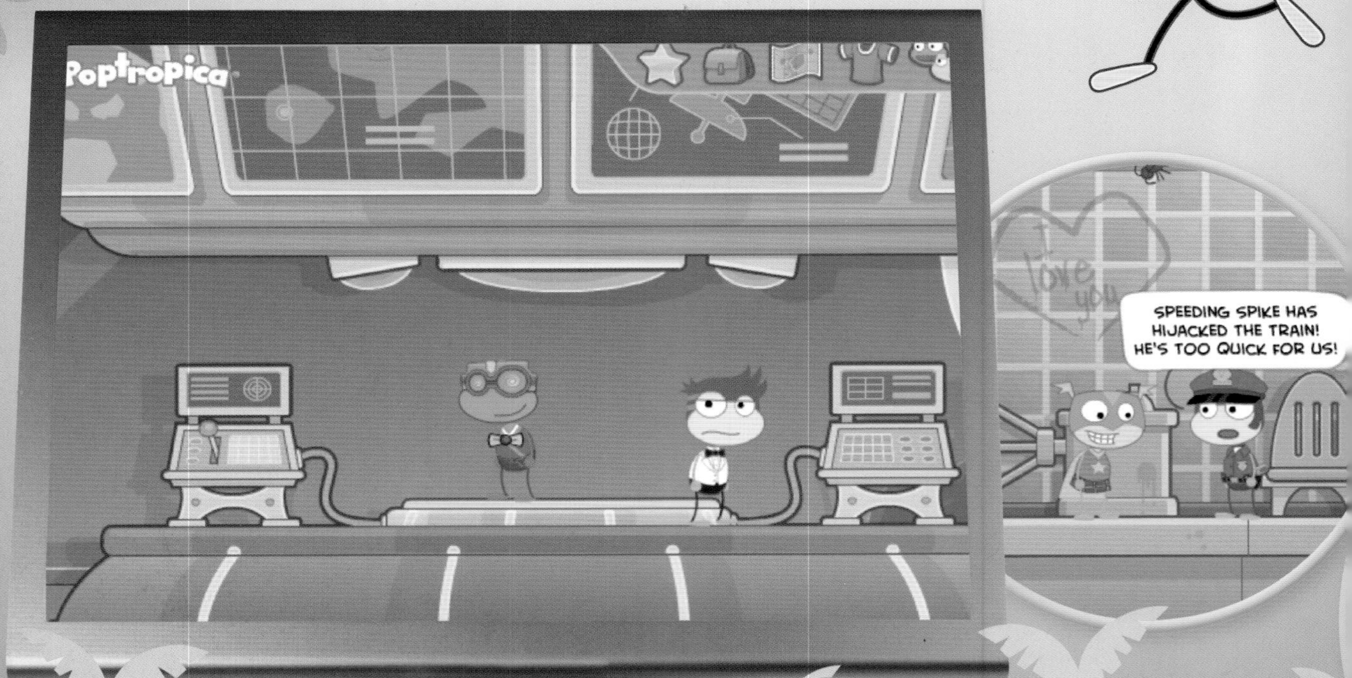
Poptropica
SPEEDING SPIKE HAS HIJACKED THE TRAIN! HE'S TOO QUICK FOR US!

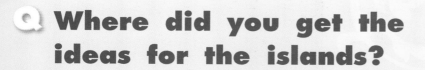

Q Where did you get the ideas for the islands?

A All sorts of places! Sometimes the first idea we come up with becomes very different in the end.

Super Power Island started because we are all fans of comic books and superhero movies. One day we said, "How can we create a story where the user can fly with super powers?" That was our starting point and everything else just fell into place.

OUT OF ORDER
WHACK!
WHACK!

Spy Island started as a joke. One of the creators, Vlad the Viking, thought it would be really funny if someone was trying to steal people's hair. The rest of the story wrote itself.

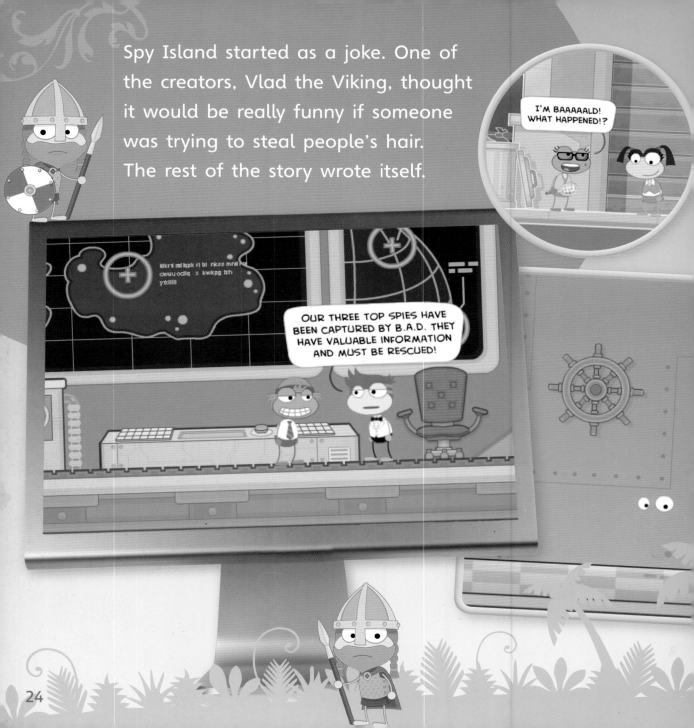

I'M BAAAAALD! WHAT HAPPENED!?

OUR THREE TOP SPIES HAVE BEEN CAPTURED BY B.A.D. THEY HAVE VALUABLE INFORMATION AND MUST BE RESCUED!

Q Which island is your favourite?

A I love Spy Island, mostly because of the bow tie and camouflage. I think they are some of the coolest items in Poptropica. You'll have to visit Spy Island to find out why!

Poptropica
Save and Quit

Q What's the best invention?

A The Medusa hair (a head with moving snakes) is funny to look at. Electrify, which lets you change the colour of your Poptropican, is another favourite. You can find these at the Poptropica store.

Poptropica
NIGHT OF THE LIVING CARROTS
CARROTS OF FIRE
OUT OF BUSINESS

Poptropica Store

Q Psst, any Poptropica secrets?

A If you dial 9-1-1 (the North American number for emergency services) into the Nabooti Island mobile phone, you get a police officer's outfit.

12345

Poptropica
BIG ZEKE'S
WILD SAFARI
BIG ZEKE'S
Save and Quit

RSHIP: BUY
CREDITS: 25
BUY MORE
Time Freeze
PUT ON
Balloons
INFLATE
Torch
TORCH
Costume Collector
USE
NEWEST | MOST POPULAR | CREATORS' PICKS | VIEW ALL | LIST VIEW
FRIES
MEMBERSHIP: BUY
CREDITS: 25
BUY MORE
GOLD CARDS
Avatar Studio
FREE
LAUNCH
Meteor Shower
USE
Snow Fall
SNOW
Haunted House
FREE
VISIT
Silly Strea
PUT ON
COSTUMES
NEWEST | MOST POPULAR | CREATORS' PICKS | VIEW ALL | LIST VIEW

Q Any more secrets?

A There's a crab on Time Tangled Island. If you click on him, he starts to twitch. See what happens when you click on him a lot!

LAB
1776 AD

Poptropica
crab

Q Best bits of the job?

A I get to work with games every day. And if someone sees me playing a computer game at work, I can say I'm doing research, and it's completely true!

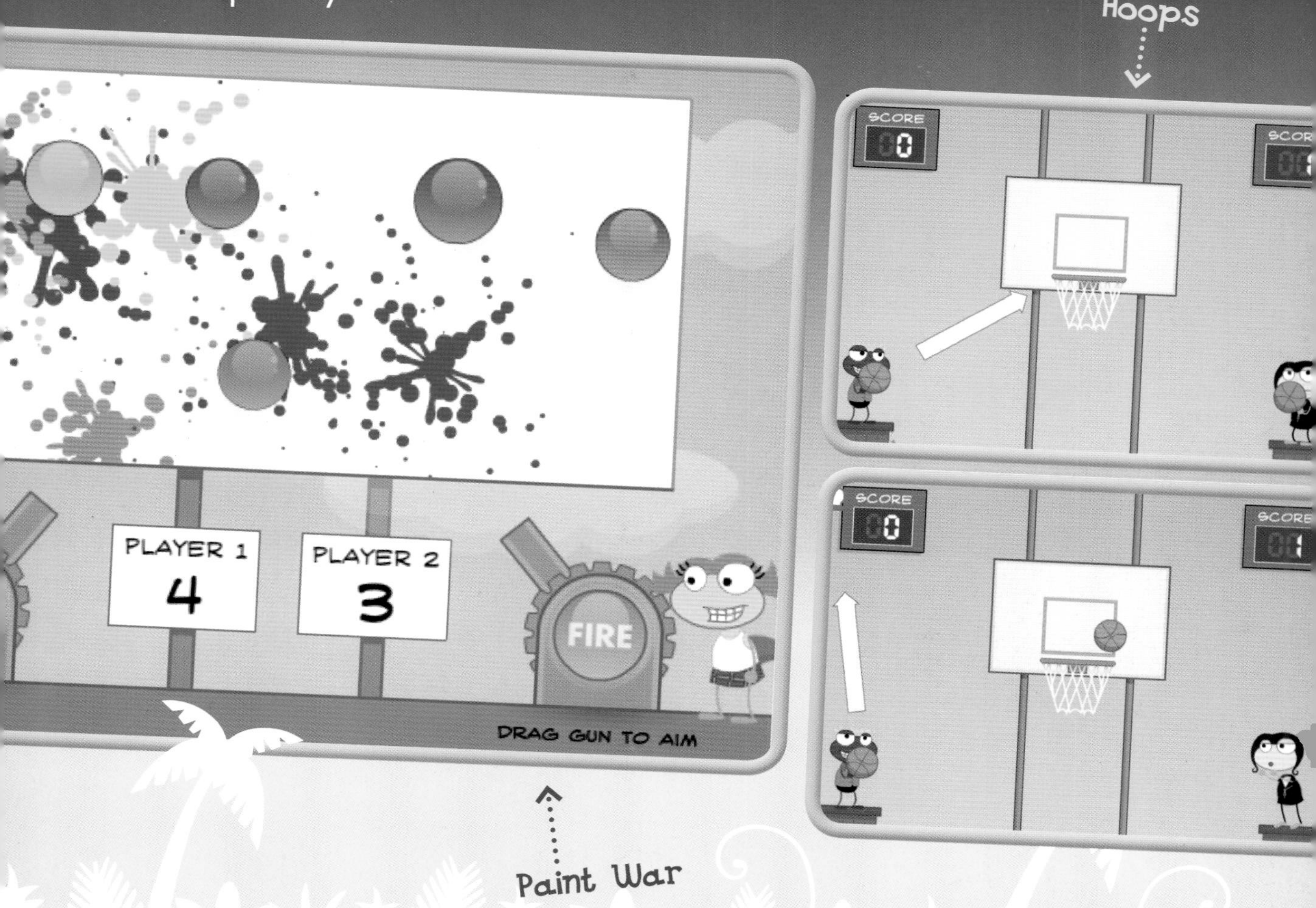
Hoops
SCORE
SCORE
SCORE
SCORE
PLAYER 1
4
PLAYER 2
3
FIRE
DRAG GUN TO AIM
Paint War

Pop Quiz

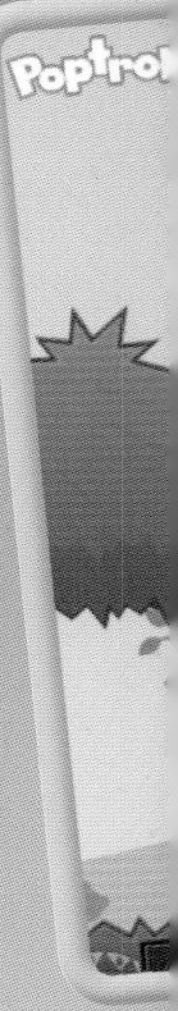

How well do you know Poptropica?

1. **How do Poptropicans travel from island to island?**

   a – by elephant

   b – by submarine

   c – by blimp

2. **True or false?**

   If you don't like your avatar's haircut, you have to wait until it grows back.

3. **Which one of these is not an island on Poptropica?**

   a – Smarty Pants Island

   b – Shark Tooth Island

   c – Time Tangled Island

4. **True or false?**

   Businesses use virtual worlds to hold meetings and sell products.

NABOOTI AFRICAN MUSEUM
Save
Poptropica CHOOSE YOUR OWN
Featured Book
TRACK STAR!
WHO ARE YOU?
WHAT IS CHOOSE YOUR OWN ADVENTURE?
CAN YOU TELL ME MORE ABOUT IT?
COME SEE ME AFTER YOU TALK TO DIRECTOR D.
club
Poptropica
Click on a player to chat or battle.
Roll over a player to view their stats.
Save

1 **c** – by blimp.

2 **False** – you can change your avatar's hair, skin colour and clothes whenever you like.

3 **a** – Smarty Pants is not an island on Poptropica.

4 **True** – virtual worlds aren't just about fun and games.

Glossary

accessories additional items, such as shoes, belts or scarves, that complement your clothes

avatar you as a computer character created online

blimp type of airship

concoction special type of mixture

credits units of value that can be used to buy things

defeat to win a victory over someone

missions quests, mystery adventures you must solve

online on the internet

personal information information that identifies you, like your name, address or school

Poptropicans name given to the avatars in Poptropica

virtual world place you can go to on the internet to chat, explore and play games against other users